OREGON COUNTY

Oregon County

Wild and Scenic

CYGNET BROWN

Ozark Grannies' Secrets

This book is dedicated to all of the wonderful people, past and present, of Oregon County, and a special thank you to my husband for his photograph used on the cover.

CONTENTS

INTRODUCTION

Introduction

Discover a county that only long-time residents are otherwise privy to. Oregon County, Missouri unites visitors with nature because it isn't rife with the commercialism of other parts of the Ozarks. If you're looking for a place where you can get back to nature, without the fluff of commercial enterprises, then Oregon County is what you're looking for. It is the home of one of only eight of the wild and scenic riverways in the United States. With this book in hand, visitors have access to the unique meshing of the geological karst topography of sinkholes, caves, canyons, and springs with diverse flora and fauna and the unique history of this part of the Ozarks. This book is a must-have for every visitor to the county who wants a deeper appreciation of the area.

The first time I came through Oregon County in 1984, I realized that I was coming home. The area was exactly what I had been looking for all my life. Its slower pace may not be for everyone, but I found it the perfect location for me to lay down my roots and raise my children.

I get it. Unlike me, most people wouldn't want to live like this all the time, but it's a wonderful place to visit, to get away from it all for a while even if you don't want to get away from the city lights permanently.

If you're looking for high-priced attractions like they have in Branson, you would be highly disappointed. Oregon County is off the beaten path and if you're looking for something unique, Oregon County offers that experience. If you're looking for high-priced, high-end hotels, you'll need to go somewhere else. If you like the idea of camping under the stars or staying in a small bed and breakfast run by locals, then you'll love Oregon County. If you're looking for a down-to-earth real-life experience, the trails, the people, the historical sites, and especially the Eleven Point River will take you back to a time when life seemed simpler.

I wrote this guide to help visitors and residents alike learn more about what this unique county has to offer. I hope you enjoy our country as well as I do.

Cygnet Brown

OREGON COUNTY

Oregon County, Missouri is located in the region called Ozark Mountains, Ozark Highlands, or sometimes the Ozark Plateau. It is a physiographic region in the U.S. states of Missouri, Arkansas, Oklahoma, and the extreme southeastern corner of Kansas. The Ozarks cover a significant portion of northern Arkansas and most of the southern half of Missouri, extending from Interstate 40 in central Arkansas to Interstate 70 in central Missouri.

It is a county located in the southern portion of the Missouri Ozarks. Its county seat is Alton. As of the 2020 census, the population was 8,635. It is surrounded by Howell County to the West, Shannon County to the North, Ripley, and Carter Counties County to the West, and the south by the Arkansas counties of Fulton, Sharp, and Randolph.

The name Ozarks may derive from an English-language adaptation of the French abbreviation aux Arcs (short for French: aux Arcansas, meaning "of/at/to the Arcansas (plural].

In the decades before the French and Indian War of 1754 to 1763, aux Arkansas referred to France's trading post at Arkansas Post, located in the wooded Arkansas Delta lowland area above the confluence of the Arkansas River with the Mississippi River.

Other possible etymological origins include French: aux arcs meaning "land of the arches", about the dozens of natural bridges formed by erosion and collapsed caves in the Ozark region. In the early 20th century, the "Ozarks" had become a widely used term for the area.

There are two mountain ranges in the Ozarks: the Boston Mountains of Arkansas and the St. Francois Mountains of Missouri. Geologically, the area is a broad dome with an exposed core in the ancient St. Francois Mountains. The Ozarks cover nearly 47,000 square miles, making it the most extensive highland region between the Appalachians and the Rockies. Together with the Ouachita Mountains, the area is known as the U.S. Interior Highlands.

Oregon County is part of the Salem Plateau, also known as the Central Plateau. The plateau is named after Salem, Missouri, and makes up the largest geologic area of the Ozarks.

Missouri is known as "The Cave State" with over 7,300 recorded caves, second in number only to Tennessee. Caves and other karst features such as springs, losing streams, and sinkholes are common in the dolomite bedrock of the Salem Plateau. The Ozark Plateaus aquifer system affects groundwater movement in all areas except the igneous core of the St. Francois Mountains.

Geographic features include limestone and dolomite glades, which are rocky, desert-like areas on hilltops. Kept open by periodic fires that limit the growth of grasses and forbs in shallow soil, glades are home to collared lizards, tarantulas, scorpions, cacti, and other species more typical of the Desert Southwest.

The topography of the Salem plateau is mostly gently rolling. The Salem Plateau is made of older Ordovician dolomites, limestones, and sandstones. Both are rife with karst topography and form long, flat plains. The formations are separated by steep escarpments that dramatically interrupt the rolling hills.

Ecology and Conservation

Formal conservation in the region began when the Ozark National Forest was created by the proclamation of President Theodore Roosevelt in 1908 to preserve 917,944 acres across five Arkansas counties. Another 608,537 acres were added the following year.

In 1939, Congress established Mark Twain National Forest at nine sites in Missouri. Wildlife management areas founded in the 1920s and '30s were created to restore populations of endangered plants and animals to viable numbers. In the 1930s and 1940s Aldo Leopold, Arthur Carhart, and Bob Marshall developed a "wilderness" policy for the Forest Service. Their efforts bore fruit with The Wilderness Act of 1964 which designated wilderness areas "where the earth and its community of life are untrammeled by men, where man himself is a visitor and does not remain". This area included second-growth public forests like the Mark Twain National Forest.

Acreage was also added to Ozark National Forest during this period. Some land was reclaimed by the government through the Resettlement Administration during the Great Depression. Protected areas ensure the recovery of endangered and threatened species of animals and plants, including the red wolf, Ozark big-eared bat, Indiana bat, eastern small-footed bat, southeastern bat, southeastern big-eared bat; longnose darter, Ozark cavefish, Ozark cave crayfish, Bowman's cave amphipod, Ozark cave amphipod, bat cave isopod; and Ozark chinquapin. It is a habitat of migratory birds and contains geological, archeological, historical, and paleontological resources.

Commercial farms and processing operations are known to raise levels of chemical and biological contaminants in Ozark streams, threatening water supplies, recreational use, and endangered native species.

Lakes and Streams

Many of the rivers and streams in the Ozarks have been dammed, but the Eleven Point River in Oregon County has been protected from that fate.

Most of the dams in the region were initially built for the dual purpose of flood control and hydropower generation but have also become major economic drivers through recreational use in places such as Branson, Missouri, and Mountain Home, Arkansas. The creation of these lakes significantly altered the Ozark landscape and affected traditional Ozark culture through displacement. The streams provided water and power to communities, farms, and mills concentrated in the valleys before impoundment. Many cemeteries, farm roads, river fords, and railways were lost when the lakes came, disrupting rural culture, travel, and commerce. Before damming, rivers and streams in the White and Osage River basins were like the current conditions of the Buffalo, Elk, Niangua, Gasconade, Big Piney, Current, Jacks Fork, Meramec, and Eleven Point rivers.

Because of the success of the Army Corps' efforts to dam the large rivers in the Ozarks, the Ozarks Society began protests to keep the other rivers in the Ozarks free flowing. The Buffalo National River (in Arkansas) was created by an Act of Congress in 1972 as the nation's first national river, administered by the National Park Service. The designation came after over a decade of battling a proposed Army Corps dam in the media, legislature, and courts to keep the Buffalo River free flowing.

In Missouri, the Ozark National Scenic Riverways was established in 1964. The Ozark National Scenic Riverways at that time included the Current and Jacks Fork Rivers which became the first US national park based on a river system. The Eleven Point River became part of the National Wild and Scenic Rivers System which was established in 1968. The parks and streams that are part of the Eleven Point National Wild and Scenic Rivers are a major economic driver for Oregon County and attract thousands of tourists annually.

Like most Ozark rivers and streams, the water of the Eleven Point River is typically clear water, with baseflows sustained by many seeps and springs, flowing through forests along limestone and dolomite bluffs. Gravel bars are common along shallow banks, while deep holes are found along bluffs. Except during periods of heavy rain or snow melt – when water levels rise rapidly – the water levels of difficulty are suitable for most canoeing and tubing.

Fish hatcheries are common due to the abundance of springs and waterways. The Missouri Department of Conservation and U.S. Fish and Wildlife Service operates numerous warm and cold-water hatcheries and trout parks and the Eleven Point is hatchery stocked every year.

Regional Economy
The area supports beef cattle ranching, and dairy farming is common across the Ozarks and there are several in the county. Dairy farms are usually cooperative affairs, with small farms selling to a corporate wholesaler, who packages products under a common brand for retail sales. Logging of primarily hardwood timber species on both private land and in the National Forests has long been an important economic activity in the county.

Most of Oregon County is forested. Oak and hickory are the predominant trees along with eastern junipers (locally referred to as cedar) and a smattering of pine trees grow in this part of the Ozarks. Less than a quarter of the region has been cleared for pasture and cropland. Forests that were heavily logged during the early-to-mid-20th century have recovered, and much of the remaining timber in the Ozarks is second-growth forest. However, deforestation of frontier forest contributed through erosion to increased gravel bars along Ozark waterways in logged areas. Stream channels have become wider and shallower, and much of the deep-water fish habitat has been lost.

Numerous rivers and streams in the past had numerous water-powered timber and grist mills. Mills were important centers of culture and commerce and were dispersed widely throughout the region. These mills served local needs, often thriving within a few miles of another facility. Few Ozark mills relied on inefficient water wheels for power; most utilized a dam, millrace, and water turbine. Several old mill sites can still be observed here in Oregon County.

During the New Deal, the Civilian Conservation Corps employed hundreds in the construction of nearly 400 fire lookouts throughout the Ozarks at 121 known sites in Arkansas and Missouri. Of those lookouts, about half remain, and many of them were used by the U.S. Forest Service. One such fire lookout can be seen on State Highway 63 in Howell County just north of the Oregon/Howell County line. A report by the National Trust for Historic Preservation deemed these fire lookouts and related structures as one of America's 11 Most Endangered Historic Places in 2007.

Current Economic Activities
Tourism is the growth industry of Oregon County as well as the rest of the Ozarks.

The trucking industry is another important industry to the regional economy. Although the national trucking companies are not based in Oregon County, numerous truck drivers live in the area.

The BNSF Railroad runs along the southern border of the county and employs several residents. Logging and timber industries are also significant in the Oregon County economy, with business concerns ranging from small family-run sawmills to large commercial operations.

Logging and sawmilling are still common income producers in the area.

Culture

"Ozark" also refers to the distinctive culture, architecture, and dialect shared by the people who live on the plateau and is notable here in Oregon County. Early settlers in this part of Missouri were pioneers who came west from the Southern Appalachians at the beginning of the 19th century, followed in the 1840s and 1850s by Irish and German immigrants. Much of the Ozark population in Oregon County descends from English, Scots Irish, and German stock. Some Ozark families in the county have lived in the area since the 19th century. One such family farm is currently on the historical record since the 1800s.

One of the first things you'll notice about Oregon County is that when you meet another car on the road if that person is from here, that person will wave at you. A lot of times, because our roads are so curvy, the driver will use just a one-finger wave, and it will be the pointer finger, not that other one-finger wave. If you stop to talk to someone, you'll be greeted with a smile and if you have any questions, you can ask anyone. They'll be happy to give you directions. If you're willing to listen, many will talk your ear off. They probably won't give you road numbers, though. Often, you'll get a description of what a turn-off looks like. If you hear the words "you can't miss it", well if you're anything like me, you probably will.

Although Oregon County residents generally adhere to socially and culturally conservative principles. They don't take kindly to people who try to change their ways.

Early settlers relied on hunting, fishing, trapping, and foraging to supplement their diets and incomes. Today hunting and fishing for recreation are common activities and an important part of the tourist industry. Foraging for mushrooms (especially morels) and ginseng is common. Other foraged plants include poke, watercress, persimmons, and pawpaw; wild berries such as blackberry, black raspberry, raspberry, red mulberry, black cherry, wild strawberry, and dewberry; and wild nuts such as black walnut and white oak acorns. Edible native legumes, wild grasses, and wildflowers are plentiful, and beekeeping is also common.

Traditional Ozark culture includes stories and tunes passed orally between generations through community music parties and other informal gatherings. Oregon County has its share of musicians. Many of these tunes and tales can be traced to British origins and German folklore. Moreover, historian Vance Randolph attributes the formation of much Ozark lore to individual families when "backwoods parents begin by telling outrageous whoppers to their children and end by half believing the wildest of these tales themselves."

Square dances were an important social avenue throughout the Ozarks into the 20th century. Square dances sprang up wherever people concentrated around mills and timber camps, springs, fords, and in towns small and large. Of all the traditional musicians in the Ozarks, the fiddler holds a distinct place in both the community and folklore. Community fiddlers were revered for carrying local tunes; regionally, traveling fiddlers brought new tunes and entertainment, even while many viewed their arrival as a threat to morality.

Religion
Ozark religion, like that of Appalachia, was predominantly Baptist and Methodist during periods of early settlement. it tends to

the conservative or individualistic. Other religious organizations include Episcopalians, Assemblies of God, Baptists including Southern Baptists, Church of Christ, Pentecostals, and other Protestant denominations present, as well as Catholics.

History

The county was organized from Ripley County on February 14, 1845. The newly formed county had a population of 750 and was named after the Oregon Territory.

The reason for the name Oregon County was simple. A live controversy was occurring between Britain and the United States over the possession of the Oregon territory, which gave rise to the slogan "Fifty-four forty or fight,". The issue was finally settled in favor of the United States in 1846. Oregon Territory was organized in 1848 and became a state in 1859.

Wild and Free During the Civil War Era

Did I mention that the people in Oregon County are individuals and like their freedom? This individualism goes way back and is demonstrated in this account from the Civil War.

In 1861, many Oregon County men joined the Missouri State Guard brigade of Judge James McBride to defend the state against what they considered to be foreigners from the north. Many did not return because they were killed at the battles of Wilson's Creek, Lexington, and Pea Ridge. In 1862 many of the survivors joined the regular Confederate Army. However, some did not approve of leaving the union and returned home. Colonel Mitchell recruited the 8th Infantry at Camp Holmes, in Thomasville. Generals Jeff Davis and Asboth came through Alton in June with their division, after General Curtis' stay in West Plains. Colonel Conrad Baker was in Thomasville in August 1862, trying to catch Dick Boze. While there, he took John R. Woodside prisoner.

Major James Wilson operated from Oregon County Courthouse for about a month from the end of September to the end of October 1863 a continued his mission of suppressing recruiting. Southern partisans then burned the Courthouse to deprive federal forces of further use of the building as headquarters. George Evans, James Harris, and Peter Younger were indicted for the crime in 1866, upon the testimony of three witnesses. Captain Robert Murphy and the Union Third Missouri State Militia were in Alton to supervise the election of November 1863.

In 1864 continuous patrols came through Oregon County. By this time both sides had to bring grain for horses and pack in other supplies because the country had been stripped bare. A court record indicated a rivalry between Captain Webster's partisans on Warm Fork and the Boze outfit on the Eleven Point River. The rivalry ended with Sterling Price's 1864 Raid in September 1864.

As the war ended in 1865 in the south and east, some local partisans had trickled back into the county, but little was left in Oregon County to interest patrols. The last action came June 15, 1865, when a patrol of the 7th Kansas sent from Pilot Knob to eradicate Devil Dick Boze, located him at the Widow Huddleston's home at Yellow Bluff on the Eleven Point River, and killed him.

Although General Lee surrendered at Appomattox Courthouse on April 9, 1865, the war had not yet ended in Oregon County. Because of a lack of interest in occupying or controlling Oregon County after Price's Raid, in 1865 lawless bands and a general disregard for any authority caused anarchy in the area. The man or group with the guns and willingness to use them ruled. Deserters, freebooters, smugglers, and thieves, both local and imported infested the hills and hollers and became powers unto themselves, especially after the last of the Federal forces moved out of Rolla,

Springfield, and Pilot Knob during the summer of 1865. Since the war started, local government dissolved and the problem exceeded the capacity of any local government to suppress. Anarchy ruled.

The outlaws plundered the few remaining locals left and sortied from hideouts to steal horses and loot the homes of anyone foolish enough to try to move back. They persistently defied attempts by local officials, whether former Confederates or northern carpetbaggers, to re-establish civil authority. Circuit court officials ventured south from Rolla and Ironton only in fear for their lives. Oregon County was especially congenial to these gangs; the sheriff himself consorted with these outlaws.

Gangs led by Jim Jamison, Dick Kitchen, Richard Boze, and other former Confederate guerrillas sheltered along the Eleven Point River near Thomasville. The former county seat of Oregon County, Thomasville had a long-established reputation along the border as a place for racing, buying, and trading fast horses. During and after the war, there were persistent rumors that it was a depot for stolen horses and a center of horse theft and smuggling with national connections through Ironton and St. Louis.

Captain William Monk from Howell County was instructed to bring order to Oregon County. William Monk was a Civil War-made man. He had been kidnapped by the southern sympathetic Missouri State Guardsmen in July 1861 and was promoted to captain of Company K or the Union 16th Missouri Cavalry. His mission was to eradicate secessionists in this part of Missouri. Monks had captured and tried to kill guerillas like Jamison and Boze in 1865 and although many outlaws were captured, the local ringleaders remained free.

Jim Jamison, a former resident of Dent County, remained in Oregon County and openly defied any effort to re-establish civil law. Radical Republican Governor Thomas Fletcher came under increasing pressure to bring the southern Missouri counties under control, and since the Missouri legislature had decreed that all men between the ages of 18 and 45 be registered in a post-war militia, he had a force to do it. In Howell County William Monks was appointed registering officer, and a major's commission in the new militia beefed up his authority. He immediately armed one hundred men, who seemed to have spent a lot of their time in Howell County ensuring former rebels they were no longer welcome there. The opposite was happening here in Oregon County.

Monks later wrote that he accepted the militia commission solely to ensure the security of Howell County from depredations of outlaws in neighboring counties and that Gov. Fletcher asked him to take command after receiving pleas from Captain John Alley, former Confederate officer and the registrar of Oregon County. Outlaws killed the returning Union veterans and threatened Captain Alley's life. They prevented him from enrolling voters according to law. Monks claimed that a secret organization of ex-Confederates known as the Sons of Liberty cooperated with the outlaws. Their united efforts were dedicated to preventing Union men from ever living in the area, by means including intimidation, robbery, arson, and murder. The outlaw chief Jim Jamison personally vowed to kill Monks if he ever entered Oregon County.

Oregon County was in a lot of trouble, and the outlaw element had to be removed. However, part of the resistance to civil authority here came from the fact that Oregon had become the opposite of Republican-controlled Howell County, it was a county of former Missouri State Guard and Confederate veterans. The problem centered on these former soldiers who were no longer allowed to vote in any election or hold public office. The Drake Constitution, passed by the Missouri Legislature in 1866, remained in effect until 1872. So, there might not have been sympathy for outlawry, but there was less for Union men coming into the county to regulate it in any way. Many of the men elected by popular vote in this time frame found themselves disqualified to hold office and were replaced by men who had received only a handful of votes.

Roving bands of outlaws still ruled Oregon and Shannon Counties in the fall of 1867. In a public gathering in the fall of 1867 in Thomasville. Colonel Jamison, one of the leaders of these outlawed bands rode into town at the head of about fifty well-armed men, shot two of the men, paraded them in the streets, and swore that if any man that attempted to enforce the civil law against them, he would face the same fate. The band rode out unmolested because the civil authorities were not willing to arrest them. A few days later, Jamison and his men rode into town. A man by the name of Philip Arbogast, owner of one of the firms of Hill-Whitmire Mercantile Company, who did business in West Plains, had been a Confederate all through the war. Arbogast told Jamison that the war was over, and he believed that the civil law ought to be enforced. Jamison dismounted, cocked his pistol, approached Arbogast, and beat him with the muzzle of his gun. He told him that if he ever heard of the man uttering a word again in favor of civil law being enforced he would hunt him down and shoot his brains out.

In another instance, two men who had been discharged from the Federal army and had once resided in Oregon County, returned to the county to look at their old homes. Colonel Jamison, with about forty men, arrested them, took them to the sheriff's house, and informed the sheriff that no "Feds" could ever reside in Oregon county, and "no damn Black Republicans could ever cast a vote at any election that was held in the county". They also informed him that they would make an example of the men as a warning to others. They said they would take them out far enough away that their stench would not annoy good Confederates. They took the men about one-half mile, stripped them naked, and shot them multiple times. They returned to the sheriff's house. with the uniforms that those men had worn in the service, their horses, a mule, and saddles which they had been riding. They gave the mule to the sheriff, took the horse with them, and published what they had done. They said that those men shouldn't be buried and that if any Confederate buried them, they would share the same fate.

Captain Alley had been a Confederate all through the war and was an honest man. He wanted to see the law enforced, and he informed Governor Fletcher of the condition of the county. Fletcher immediately appointed him as the enrolling officer for the county. Fletcher ordered Captain Alley to enroll and organize the county into militia companies. He was to form a posse to aid the sheriff in enforcing the law. As soon as he received his commission, he rode into the different townships and put up his notices requesting the residents meet him to enroll in militia companies.

Jamison, with about forty men, rode into the township where the first meeting was to be and posted another written notice on the same tree, when Captain Alley, the old, white-headed man, appeared to carry out the orders of the Governor, Jamison himself would meet Captain Alley and shoot his old head off his shoulders. Alley, being satisfied that he would carry out his threat, went to the place before daylight and concealed himself nearby. About 10 o'clock that day, Jamison and about 40 followers charged in on their horses revolvers in hand. They cursed and declared that they would like to see the "old white-headed scoundrel" put in an appearance so they could make an example of him. They did not intend to let any man enforce the law against them.

Meanwhile, Monks took the Howell County arm of the Missouri State Militia to Oregon County in the fall of 1867. It was a brutal campaign. When the militiamen captured four of Jim Jamison's cohorts, Monks had them lashed to a wagon. At the same time, he sent word to the outlaw that he would kill the prisoners if Jamison's men fired upon the militia. Monks then proceeded into the outlaw's lair, but Jamison and his gang elected not to test his resolve. Later, some of his militiamen captured the Oregon County sheriff and tortured him by hanging him until he was ready to talk. The militia however did not limit their activities to eradicating outlaws and in many cases, these men spent their time hunting for former Confederate enemies to settle old scores. The situation went so bad for the newly resurrected Oregon County Circuit Court that it raised its militia to hunt down the outlaws so they would have reason to get Monks to leave.

Two companies of Oregon County militiamen, nearly all ex-Confederate soldiers, joined the Howell County company, and the combined battalion dispersed the criminals. Some were captured and turned over to civil authorities for trial. The Oregon County militia tracked and when found, killed others. Jim Jamison and Dick Kitchen left Missouri altogether. Later Jamison joined the Texas Rangers and received a pardon for his war crimes from Missouri's governor. Others fled to Indian Territory where they expected to evade the reach of justice, only to swing later on Judge Isaac Parker's gallows at Fort Smith, Arkansas.

The Oregon County militiamen probably did the lion's share of the work. Captain Alley wrote the Adjutant General of Missouri in 1867 that Monks's company was not doing much and stated that he would not be displeased to see it move on. Monks finally took his company north into Shannon County to prevent the gangs from escaping in that direction. The State Militia detachment was relieved from active service in December 1867. In 1868, the Oregon County court reconvened. Monks complained that the ringleaders had been killed or driven out but left behind sympathizers.

At that time, a secret order in the counties of Oregon and Shannon existed known as the Sons of Liberty. On a certain night, authorities discovered that the Sons of Liberty would hold a meeting on the Warm fork of Spring River. Monk's men made a forced march and, on reaching the place where they had assembled, surrounded the house, and made them prisoners. Among them were the county sheriff and other prominent men. The next morning Captain Alley met Monk and put up his notices ordering every man to come in and enroll his name. The next day, Monk had their papers, with a secret oath placed upon them, and the aims and objects, binding themselves together to prevent the enforcement of the civil law, and further bond themselves to capture or take property from any man who had been in the Federal army, and, when they needed to enforce it, they shot men down. They claimed to have lawyers connected with it, and that if they were arrested they would make a pretense of a trial and allow no man to go onto the jury except those who belonged to the order.

Captain Greer, who had been a captain in the Confederate service all through the war, and afterward was elected to the state legislature, remarked that "I can soon tell whether those grips, obligations and oaths were in the organization known as the Sons of Liberty;" Uncle Dickey Boles had recently come to him and informed him that the Sons of Liberty were going to hold a meeting in a big sink on the mountain and they wanted him to come and join them. He told him that they saw him as a businessman, but he didn't know anything about what was going on right at his door. He was told that if he would come and join the organization, in a few years he would be a rich man. Captain Greer said he replied, "Uncle Dickey, I have always been an honest man and have worked hard, and if a man can get rich in two or three years by joining that order, there must be something dishonest in it."

Old Uncle Dickey replied; "You won't be in a bit of danger in joining it, for we are so organized that the civil law can't reach us."

Captain Greer said he had a son-in-law who received the same invitation to attend the meeting. After the meeting, he saw Captain Greer and asked him what kind of an organization it was.

He said his son-in-law told him, "I dare not tell you; I took the bitterest oath that I have ever taken in my life not to reveal the workings of the order on penalty of death. But I will tell you enough, Captain, I know that you are an honest man and that that organization is a damn jay-hawking institution, and you want nothing to do with it."

Captain Greer at once sent for his son-in-law; he came, and the signs, grips, and by-laws that were captured at the place of the meeting were submitted to him and he said he believed they were word for word the same, and contained the very same oath that they swore him to on the night that he went to their meeting.

As the gunfire subsided by 1870, the war of words continued for at least another decade. The political struggle played itself out in regional races like Circuit Judge. It was with delight that Colonel John R. Woodside defeated William Monks in the early 1870's. In the immediate post-war period, while the radical Republicans, numerous criminal indictments were filed against former rebels seeking compensation for stolen horses and property. Monks filed civil suits against his former kidnappers and in some cases took their property. After the radical Republicans fell out of power the tables turned and indictments were filed in Monk's home county charging him with murder. On one occasion while Monks was appearing in a neighboring county court he had to jump through a window and ride away to avoid a young man he had mistreated during the war killing him with a shotgun.

Some rebel sympathizers remained in the county. The only weapons they had were their tongues. having no conscience or principle, and instigated by the wicked one, they began lying and preferring all manner of charges against Monk and his men who went into the county and, by the aid of the law-abiding citizens, drove out and arrested one of the worst set of men that ever lived, the savage not excepted, and restored the civil law, so that every citizen was secure in person and property.

This independent thinking continues to this day. These are a few of the historical events that are found here in Oregon County, Wild and Scenic.

THE ELEVEN POINT RIVER

The Eleven Point River is one of Oregon County's finest and best-known features. The scenery along the Eleven Point River is exemplary within the region of comparison. Numerous attributes meld together to create attractive and distinctive scenery, including the concentration of unique geologic features, the rich composition of plant communities, and the distinct water characteristics.

Natural Features

This is the most important stream in the county. It rises in Howell County, where it is called Eleven Points Creek It crosses Oregon County from northwest to southeast, and flows into Arkansas, where it unites with Spring River, and finally empties into Black River.

The composition of the existing geology is unique as it was deposited as a calcium-rich limestone, and due to its original properties and the changing depositional environment, a rare process known as dolomitization changed the composition to a magnesium-rich rock. The magnesium ions are easily dissolved in the mildly acidic rainwater, allowing for most of the annual precipitation to infiltrate the formation providing an abundance of ground water and highly recharged springs. Nearby caves that are above the surface and accessible to humans and wildlife are considered "inactive;" the same hydrogeologic processes currently taking place, known as karst, are forming "active" caves in the subsurface opening large voids for water to move sediments through.

History

The name of Eleven Point River is an old one. Robert Hatcher, one of the very early pioneers settled near the current town of Thomasville around 1814 according. Another account claims he settled on Eleven Points River in 1816. Yet another report states that the first settlement was made in 1803 by Charles Hatcher. The area that was settled became known as Mill Hollow because Oliver Longgreer operated a lumber and planing mill there from about 1884 to 1892. Hatcher Spring, now Posey Spring was one mile up the hollow.

Historically, the Eleven Point River was a prime route into the area by those who settled in southeast Missouri. The river provided power for mills, transported timber, deposited rich agricultural soils, and offered productive hunting and fishing. Before railroad infrastructure in this area, rivers made commerce beyond individual subsistence possible. Towns grew around the mills, and commerce thrived wherever industrious settlers chose to put down roots. The Eleven Point River and its settlers also played vital roles and suffered great losses during the American Civil War, and the evidence of these tumultuous times is still present in the river bottoms, foothills, and ridges above the Eleven Point River. The Greer Mill is a perfect example of one such historic property within the river corridor that has stood the test of time and has become a cornerstone in the heritage of the people who live here today.

The Forest Service, in partnership with many other cooperators and volunteers, has fully restored the Greer Mill and stabilized the dam at Boze Mill. They created visitor-use paths around Thomasson Mill.

A pioneer grist mill set up before the Civil War by Mr. Ferguson, known by his name Ferguson Mill. Soon after the war Jack

Thomason from Tennessee bought the farm and mill. Later the mill was purchased in 1937 by William Sheers, a merchant of St. Louis, and operated by S.S. Williams. Besides meal, flour, and stock feed grinding, cotton is also ginned.

Prehistory
Pre-European-contact history along the Eleven Point Scenic River is very important. Archeologists have found a variety of use patterns during the Archaic Period (9,000 to 3,000 years ago) and continuing into the Woodland Period through European contact. Out of the 53 sites recorded with pre-contact components, only 9 sites are considered ineligible for inclusion in the National Register of Historic Places (NRHP). The remaining 44 precontact sites within the surveyed corridor are all considered eligible for inclusion on the NRHP pending further work to determine otherwise. The designated corridor provides ideal conditions for the preservation of currently undisturbed archaeological remains.

Pre-European-contact history along the Eleven Point Scenic River is very important. Archeologists have found a variety of use patterns during the Archaic Period (9,000 to 3,000 years ago) and continuing into the Woodland Period through European contact. Out of the 53 sites recorded with pre-contact components, only 9 sites are considered ineligible for inclusion in the National Register of Historic Places (NRHP). The remaining 44 precontact sites within the surveyed corridor are all considered eligible for inclusion on the NRHP pending further work to determine otherwise. The designated corridor provides ideal conditions for the preservation of currently undisturbed archaeological remains.

The River's Uniqueness
Of the 45 rivers in Missouri, only three are classified as federally protected scenic rivers. These protected rivers are under two

different acts of Congress, so they are managed under two different scenic river systems. The Current River and Jacks Fork are a part of the protected Ozark National Scenic Riverways Act of 1964 and are managed by the NPS. Only the Eleven Point River is part of the protected Wild and Scenic Rivers System Act of 1968 and is managed by the United States Forest Service. All are ideal for secluded backcountry camping, great fishing, and breathtaking float trips. These pristine Missouri Scenic Rivers are generally crystal clear except during and after heavy rains usually occurring in the spring. They are all spring-fed and maintain a constant temperature of 62-68 degrees F. year-round. The average temps of the spring sources that feed the rivers are even colder at an average of 56 degrees F.

The Eleven Point River is a 138-mile-long river in southern Missouri and northern Arkansas. The river originates near Willow Springs, Missouri in Howell County. but in Oregon County It more than doubles in flow when Greer Spring Branch runs into it, adding over 200 million US gallons of water per day to the river. The name "Eleven Point" derives from the Mississippi Valley French word 'pointe', which is a wooded point of land marking a river bend. Voyageurs marked distance by counting these points of land or river bends. The river empties into the Spring River southwest of Pocahontas near the small town of Black Rock, Arkansas.

Most of the Eleven Point River meanders through Oregon County. The river enters Oregon County at the Howell/Oregon County line just west of Thomasville and heads due east through the Cane Bluff area past the Wilderness area, down to Greer Spring where it grows considerably. From there it heads south through the Turners Mill area, through Whitten, Riverton, and through to the narrows and the State Road 142 access. At 142, the Eleven Point widens again. From there it continues to the Myrtle access and then continues down into Arkansas where it eventually flows into the Spring River.

To the experienced canoeist, the Eleven Point is a relatively easy river (Class I and Class II) requiring intermediate experience. Snags, trees, and root wads remain the most dangerous of all obstacles and on occasion may require scouting from shore. Although canoes are the time-tested means of travel on the Eleven Point River, kayaks are increasingly common, and flat-bottom john boats, primarily for fishing trips, are used on the river. You may encounter boats with motors; motorboats are restricted to a 25-hp limit. Particularly during the late summer, you may also encounter some float tubes, but the cold water and longer distances between river accesses limit this use.

Smallmouth bass, rock bass, walleye, and trout are eagerly sought by anglers on the Eleven Point. A trout permit is also required if you fish trout. Gigging is popular, but not permitted within the Wild Trout Management Area.

THE ONLY WILD AND SCENIC
RIVER IN MISSOURI

In 1968 a 44.4-mile stretch of the Eleven Point was named the Eleven Point National Wild and Scenic River, one of the original eight rivers chosen to be part of the United States National Wild and Scenic Rivers System.

The National Wild and Scenic Rivers System was created by the Wild and Scenic Rivers Act of 1968 (Public Law 90-542[1]), enacted by the U.S. Congress to preserve certain rivers with outstanding natural, cultural, and recreational values in a free-flowing condition for the enjoyment of present and future generations.

Designated rivers are assigned one or more classifications: Wild, Scenic, or Recreational. These classifications are based on the developmental character of the river's surroundings on the date of designation. Wild rivers are the most remote and undeveloped while Recreational rivers often have many access points, roads, railroads, bridges, and homes located within the designated corridor. Scenic rivers tend to fall somewhere between the Wild and Recreational levels of development. It is important to note that a river's classification is not related to the value(s) that made it worthy of designation. For instance, recreation may not be an outstanding value on a river with a recreational classification, nor scenery on a river classified as scenic. Notably, Wild and Scenic Rivers receive the same protection standard regardless of classification.

The Act protects the special character of these rivers, while also recognizing the potential for their appropriate use and development. The law encourages river management to cross political boundaries and encourages the public to participate in developing goals for river protection. President Lyndon B. Johnson signed the act into law.

United States rivers were preserved with several designations. All were designated for possessing outstandingly remarkable values (ORVs). The selected rivers fall into the 8 categories: Scenic, Recreation, Geologic, Fish, Wildlife, Historic, Culture, or Other similar values. These values can be considered synonymous with ecosystem services, or those goods and services that nature provides freely and that ultimately benefit society. Rivers (or sections of rivers) so designated are set out for protection and enhancement in perpetuity by preserving their free-flowing condition from dams and development that would otherwise diminish the quality of their remarkable values. National Wild and Scenic designation essentially veto the licensing of new dams on, or directly affecting the designated section of the river. It also provides strong protection against federally funded bank and channel alterations that adversely affect river values, protects riverfront public lands from new oil, gas, and mineral development, and creates a federal reserved water right to protect flow-dependent values such as fish habitat.

The Eleven Point River is one of the original eight rivers named under the Wild and Scenic Rivers Act as possessing "outstandingly remarkable scenic, recreational, geologic, fish and wildlife, historic, cultural or other similar values." The Eleven Point holds the scenic designation within the National Wild and Scenic Rivers system, meaning that it is free of impoundments, with shorelines or watersheds still largely primitive and shorelines largely undeveloped, but accessible in places by roads. The river wasn't always wilderness, many old homesites, fences, farms, and roads were located along the river, but in only a few decades have since been reclaimed by nature. Half of the land in the designated area is public and owned by the National Forest Service. The government holds a scenic easement on other land within the area that preserves its character for the future but does not allow public access to privately held land.

In addition to the Eleven Point—Clearwater, Feather, Rio Grande, Rogue, St Croix, Salmon, and Wolf Rivers were designated as National Wild and Scenic Rivers. Only the Eleven Point is in Missouri. This designation as a Wild and Scenic River specifically protects the free-flowing nature of rivers in both federal and non-federal areas, something the Wilderness Act and other federal designations cannot do. Despite misplaced fears, the WSR designation did not alter private property rights.

Four principal land managing agencies of the federal government manage National Wild and Scenic Rivers. Most National Wild and Scenic Rivers, including the Eleven Point, are managed by the United States Forest Service, followed by the National Park Service; ten of those managed by the NPS are official units, while most are part of other parks. The remaining WSR are managed under the Bureau of Land Management's National Conservation Lands, originally called the National Landscape Conservation System, and the U.S. Fish and Wildlife Service in Alaska.

The designated part of the Eleven Point River stretches from Thomasville through Cane Bluff, Greer, Turners Mill, through Riverton, to State Highway 142, the entire portion that runs through Oregon County.

The Eleven Point River is best experienced by boat. Canoeing is extremely popular. Jon boating is frequently used by fishermen. Smallmouth bass, rock bass, walleye, and trout are some of the game fish fished from the river. Float camps are minimally developed along the river and accessible by boat, and dispersed camping on gravel bars is allowed.

THE ELEVEN POINT SECTION OF
THE OZARK TRAIL

Eleven Point River section of the Ozark Trail in Oregon County Missouri runs east and west about 20 miles south of Winona, Missouri. Several lookout points are along the Eleven Point River. *Leffer Look* has high bluffs from which to gaze at the water. *Devil's Backbone* offers karst features. Another point of interest along the Eleven Point River Section of the Ozark Trail is the history at *Bockman Spring House* and the cool waters of Hurricane Creek. *Greer Spring* is also just on the south side of the river! The trail leaves the 3152 trailhead, winding along the side slopes to Hurricane Creek. (Warning: The crossing is dangerous during high water.)

The first ten miles pass through very rugged slopes and flowages associated with the Eleven Point National Scenic River. Several fine views of the Eleven Point valley are present. From the Greer Recreation area, at mile 10, the trail parallels the Eleven Point River on its way to McCormack Lake. There is a fine picture opportunity at the mouth of Greer Spring and an excellent bluff view of the river near mile 12. A spur leads to *McCormack Lake* at mile 13. Continuing west, the trail winds through the rugged Eleven Point terrain and offers two more contacts with the river. Near mile 20, the trail passes next to *Bockman Spring*, which is part of the Spring Creek flowage.

The westernmost ten miles of the trail are in the *Spring Creek* flow area and offer occasional views of the creek and bottom fields. Four trailheads occur on this section: From Winona, take Highway 19 south to FS 3152. Go east about six miles to the trailhead.

For an amazing hike, check out white's Creek Trail. The Adventure begins at the Five Pond Trailhead and can be accessed off County Road J in Fremont, Missouri.

As you turn off County Road J, prepare to be awestruck by the impressive pine-tree-lined road leading to Camp Five Pond parking lot one.

Most hikers recommend going counterclockwise (right at the fork) when hiking White's Creek Trail. Here are the trails that you will encounter when following this route--Bliss Spring (8 miles from the trailhead) White's Creek (about 6 miles past Bliss Spring) – the trail's namesake – with its clear blue water and ending with Fiddler's Spring.

If you're looking for a shorter day hike, consider going clockwise to Fiddler's Spring and back.

Bliss Spring is the first water source on White's Creek Trail and feeds into the Eleven Point River. Next, you'll come to White's Creek Trail about six miles past Bliss Spring trail that runs along White's Creek. Here's a great place to take a break to enjoy the view and explore White's cave on the other side of the water. Finally, at the trail's end, you'll come to Fiddler's Spring for another refreshing stop.

THE ELEVEN POINT RIVER ACCESSES

In addition to the Eleven Point Section of the Ozark Trail, there are also numerous ways to enjoy the river while on the water.

Thomasville River Access

Thomasville River Access, situated in Oregon County, provides the first opportunity for accessing the Eleven Point National Scenic River. State Highway 99 bridge is the put-in point for river access.

This location provides an amazing float trip down the river from Thomasville to either Cane Bluff (9.3 miles) or the Greer Access (16.6 miles). This section of the river can usually be floated from March through June. Motorized boats are not recommended in this portion of the river.

While floating you will be able to view nature at its best especially if you take the float in spring. Beautiful flowers, tall shady trees, and graceful wildlife are seen everywhere. The water flows clear and unpolluted from more than thirty major springs that feed it constantly and produce year-round paddling conditions. Some spots will require walking and/ or portages as the river is not deep in some places, particularly during droughts.

The rapids on the river are generally classified as Class 1 and 2. A generous variety of fish live in the river. Everything from crayfish to largemouth bass can be caught. Check state regulations for fishing due to certain fishing limitations.

Cane Bluff River Access

A perpendicular bluff, about 600 ft. high, on Eleven Points River. It is covered with dense cane growth. Nearby was the Cane Bluff Ford. This river crossing was part of an old pioneer trail that led from Pocahontas to Thomasville. Thomas Bowles of Alton built a clubhouse there about 1923. It burned a few years later.

Leading into Eleven Points River, near Cave Bluff was Bone Hollow, also known as Huddleston Hollow, Peggy Hollow, and Bozo Hollow. During the Civil War guerilla hands marauded this section and several persons were killed one evening when a dance at Aunt "Peggy" Huddleston's home was disturbed. It is said that the people fled, and some bodies were left unburied, their bones remaining in the valley. Richard ("Devil Dick") Boze, a guerilla leader, was killed. Superstitious individuals always believed the place was haunted and no one would live in the Huddleston house for some years.

Cane Bluff River Access is located on the left side of the Eleven Point National Scenic River. This upper section of the river is small and is comfortably floated in the spring season. Cane Bluff Access is unimproved with a toilet along a scenic stretch of river with towering rock bluffs.

Cane Bluff Access has a concrete boat ramp, picnic tables, and restrooms along a scenic stretch of river with towering rock bluffs. The gravel access road off Highway 19 is rough in places and has a low water bridge across a shallow spring branch.

Greer Recreation Area

Greer Recreation Area can be reached by driving from Winona, Missouri by taking Highway 19 south to the Eleven Point River. It can also be reached from Alton by driving North on Missouri Highway 19 to the Eleven Point River.

You exit the highway to the campground to the left with camp-sites located off a road that circles through the campground. If you stay straight you will get to the boat launch and day-use area.

This campground is primarily used by people using the river. It's a nice flat, level area immediately adjacent to the highway. This campground is a hub that puts you in the vicinity of Greer Mill, Greer Spring, and numerous other historic mills and springs in the area. These sites are not within walking distance but are a reasonable drive away along Highway 19.

When you access the site from the river, it is located on the right-hand side. You'll exit the highway, the campground is located to the left with campsites located off of a loop road that circles through the campground. If you stay straight you will get to the boat launch and day-use area.

This campground is primarily used by people using the river. It's a nice flat, level area immediately adjacent to the highway.

This campground is a hub that puts you in the vicinity of Greer Mill, Greer Spring, and numerous other historic mills and springs. There are several historic sites in the area also. These sites are not within walking distance but are a reasonable drive away along Highway 19.

When you access the site from the river, it will be located on the right-hand side.
The campground is set back away from the water's edge. A campground host is on-site in the summer. Sites, which offer seclusion and privacy, each with a table, fire ring, and lantern post.

A picnic area is near the boat access. This boating access is one of the most popular launch sites for people floating the Eleven Point.

There is one trail available for hikers; a 4-mile trail that follows the river and through typical Ozark hills up to McCormack Lake then circles back for a 2-mile walk back to Greer. This trail runs along the river and then back along the hillside above the river.

Rainbow trout, small-mouth bass, and sunfish are among the fishing opportunities at this location.

Greer Spring

The entrance to the trail to Greer Spring is about half a mile south of the Greer Recreation Area. When you pull into the parking lot it's easy to find the trailhead which starts you on the downhill, 0.9-mile hike to Greer Spring. Don't forget to stop at the restroom before you head down the hill. Even though it's a short hike, bring plenty of water to drink, especially in the summer months.

Greer Spring is the second largest spring in Missouri. Greer Spring flows from two outlets about 250 feet apart at the bottom of a steep, shaded ravine at the terminus of the trail. More like the emergence of an underground river, the water feeding Greer Spring comes from nearby streams that flow underground, as well as sinkholes found to the west and northwest of the spring, as far as 35 miles away.

The spring flows from the mouth of Greer Spring Cave, which is the mouth of the spring branch, and boils up from the rugged bed of the stream. The spring run drops 62 feet in elevation for 1.25 miles where it more than doubles the flow of the Eleven Point National Scenic River where they join.

The 0.9-mile trail to the spring travels through a mixture of hardwoods and pines. The overstory of trees includes a variety of oaks, shortleaf pine, hickory, maples, basswood, and black gum.

In the spring, hikers will also see flowering dogwoods, sassafras, persimmon, hazelnuts, cedar, and hackberry trees.

Rock formations along the spring and spring branch canyons inspire many photographers. Flowing down a rock-filled canyon for one mile, the spring branch enters the Eleven Point River. There is no fishing, boating, floating, or wading allowed in the spring branch.

White's Creek and Cave
This float camp is on the Western side of the Irish Wilderness and provides access to the Whites Creek Trail system.

White's Creek flows into Eleven Points River. It was named after a pioneer family of the name "White" who lived there before the Civil War. White's Cave in the valley is the largest in Oregon County.

White's Creek and cave can be found in the Wilderness and can be accessed from J Highway in Ripley County as part of the White's Creek Trail.

The Whites Creek Float Camp is located on the left side of the Eleven Point National Scenic River. This camp is just 0.5 miles below Whitten and is only accessible by boat. This is a primitive campsite at the mouth of White's Creek with a pit toilet.

This is a primitive campsite only accessible by the river, Whitten is the closest upriver site and Riverton East is the next takeout downriver.

Turners Mill River Accesses
Located on the edge of the Irish Wilderness area near Alton, Missouri, Turner Spring has a 1.5-million-gallon average daily flow. The spring flows from a high rocky bluff. The remains of the mill

wheel are located on the north side of the Eleven Point River adjacent to Turner's Spring.

During the late 1880s or early 1890s Jesse L. Clay Turner, from Tennessee, homesteaded 160 acres on Eleven Points River, thus securing ownership of the spring. About 1895, he bought from the Hardin brothers the ruins of the old Williams Mill and put it repaired it.

Later he put in a sawmill and operated a store. For a time, he operated a toll bridge. A post office called Surprise was established in 1895 and remained in operation until 1925. When the post office was established, Turner gave the name Surprise, saying people would be surprised at what a well-improved, good place he was developing. After his death, his mill and the town went into ruins and the post office was discontinued, but the spring remains strong and beautiful.

Turner Mill North Eleven Point River access is located on the north side of the Eleven Point National Scenic River. This access is 4.9 miles downriver of Greer Crossing. The next access downriver from Turner Mill is Whitten.

Turner's Mill North access road from Missouri Highway 19 going north from Alton and past the Greer access. Turn right onto FR 3152 for 6 miles then turn right on FR 3190 for 3 miles. The site is at the end of the road.

There is no camping on the North side of the River. The North River Access is strictly for viewing and exploring.

Turner Mill South can be accessed from the south side of the Eleven Point River. This access is rustic and offers limited dispersed campsites, limited day-use area, a single-lane concrete boat launch, and toilet facilities. The South Turner's Mill Access Road is just off Missouri Highway AA.

To locate the South Turner's Mill access, take Hwy 19 north for 2 miles to Hwy AA, turn right/east onto AA, and travel 4 miles to County 127/Forest Service Road 3153. Turn left onto County Road 127/Forest Service Road 3153 and drive about 4 miles to the Turner Mill South access.

On this road can be found Cate's Pond Church, formerly known as Bildad Baptist Church. This church was built five or six years before the Civil War, the United Baptists built, near the present site, a house of hewed logs to be used for church and school. The name was chosen because it was the name of one of Job's three friends. Gilbert Williams, who came from Tennessee in 1853, suggested the name.

The church was organized by two ministers of the settlement-- Thomas C. Simpson and Jeff Sisco. When this building burned in 1884, a house was erected about two miles south and used for church by the Baptists and Methodists and for school.

The Methodists, disbanding during the early 1920s, sold their interests to the Freewill Baptists who then built a church near Cates Pond but retained their old name. The name of Bildad is a strange selection among Bible characters to use for a church, for he was one of the three friends of whom Job declared, "Miserable comforters are ye all" (16:2), and he made a point of deriding Job's long speeches: "How long will it be ere ye make an end of words?" (18:2). Some at least of the congregation were aware of the incongruity of the name, which must have been conferred in a humorous spirit, is shown by the following anecdote. Because of the long sermons and additional talks at the old, early church, a local, derisive expression;

"Well, they Billdad us through" developed and for years was still used when services are unusually long and tiresome.

The Forest Service maintains a recreation site and the historic single-room Surprise School at Turners Mill. Surprise School underwent a major stabilization in 2018 after the 2017 flood nearly destroyed the structure. It is a rare example of a single-room schoolhouse that is a characteristic symbol of an American community in the late 19th and early 20th centuries.

Whitten River Access

Whitten River Access is twelve miles east of Alton off Missouri AA Highway. The Ozark Land and Lumber Company gave the site its name. It was named for Drew Whitten, who owned land and lived near when a school was established in the early 1900s.

Today, the Whitten River Access is located on the right bank of the Eleven Point National Scenic River. This is a popular launch and take-out site on the river. There is a vault toilet and single-lane concrete boat ramp located at this access site.

Visitors enjoy the 11-mile float from Greer downriver to Whitten. The area is busy on weekends with both motorized and non-motorized users. From Whitten is another popular day float allowing visitors to travel downriver eight miles from Whitten to Riverton.

Boze Mill Access

Boze Mill was a pioneer grist mill on Eleven Points River north of Riverton. It was built as early as 1850 by Richard Boze ("Devil Dick" Boze), and his brother. Mr. B.N. Jones of Riverton had the old corn burrs that had the patent stamp of 1831, which Mr. Casey thought are not the original burrs used there. The spellings "Bose" and

"Bows" were found on some maps, but a granddaughter of Richard Boze gives the "z" spelling. Later the mill came into possession of Marshall Boze. The mill was an important center of commerce where farmers could get wheat and corn ground into flour. Then it was owned by James Conner. During the middle 1880s, Clelland Mitchell of Bardley (formerly of St. Louis), bought the old wooden mill, and then in 1902 Morgan Woodring bought it from the Mitchell heirs, after which he put in a concrete dam.

Today, Boze Mill Spring forms a sparkling blue pool that produces between 12-14 million gallons of water per day. Aquatic plants add many shades of green to the spring branch. Boze Mill is nestled in a beautiful glen beside the Eleven Point River just above Riverton. The historical 1880s turbine and hand-layered rock wall from the Lucas Boze grist mill still exist today.

The mill site can be reached by road or by river. It is a popular stopping place for canoers of the Eleven Point River. A primitive campsite allows for camping. A vault toilet is centrally located.

Wade or float fishing is allowed for rainbow trout, bass, and pan fish. Be aware however that the extremely cold water and swift current may make wading hazardous.

To get to Boze Mill by road, from Riverton, go east on Hwy 160, turn left/north onto County Road 152, and travel for 2 miles to Boze Mill Spring on your left.

Travelers who arrive by road can park at the trailhead and walk to the river access and picnic area. Tables and grills are available. If you are floating into the camp, the access stream is between Whitten upriver and Riverton East.

Riverton River Access

Riverton is located on U.S. Route 160 on the west side of the crossing over the Eleven Point River. Riverton was founded in the 1920s and was named after Riverton, Wyoming.

Riverton was a good crossing for hunting and fishing. Charles R. Jones, from Stoddard County, put in the first store in 1923. He gave the name of Riverton, Wyoming, where he had operated a store for a short time. The name, meaning a town on the river, is quite appropriate.

The Riverton River Access provides restrooms and day camping facilities only as well as a boat ramp.

About six and a half miles north of Riverton is Stillhouse Hollow which leads into the Eleven Point River. Before the Civil War, a twelve-foot still was built here where they continued making whiskey during the war. After prohibition was established much moonshine whiskey was made in this thinly settled region.

Another spring in another location was called Stillhouse Spring. The name originated from a large still operated there before the Civil War by a landowner, Solomon Depriest, who had come from Illinois.

The Riverton River Access is located thirteen miles from Alton, Missouri on Missouri Highway 160.

Highway 142/Narrows River Access-

The Highway 142 access, also known as "The Narrows", is the last river access for the Eleven Point National Scenic River. This access is 8.7 miles downriver of Riverton. This is a developed site with a single-lane, concrete boat ramp, paved parking, and a vault toilet.

Floaters can put in at the Riverton access float the eight miles and take out at Highway 142 Access.

It is a quick drive over to Morgan Springs Float Camp parking where you can hike to Morgan Spring. These springs are in a beautiful area called the "Narrows," which gets its name from a narrow ridge of land between the river and Frederick Creek.

Two large springs of bluish water are located near "The Narrows". One of the beautiful spots of unusual scenery near Eleven Points River The scenery in its natural wildness is breathtaking if you're willing to hike up to the summit. The smaller one, generally known as Blue Spring on land that in 1937 was owned by Mrs. W.L. Caldwell near Billmore School. Its estimated daily flow is from 17,000,000 to 32,000,000 gallons. The larger one is also known as Thomason Mill Spring. Its estimated flow is 43,000,000 gallons.

Blue Spring, also known as Billmore Spring can best be accessed if you go upstream from Riverton and paddle to the creek that leads back to the spring. You could reach it from Whitten but are likely to miss the entrance because you'll be close to the Riverton access by that time.

OREGON COUNTY COMMUNITIES-PAST AND PRESENT

ALTON

Alton is at the county's center and is the county seat. The population was 707 at the 2020 census. It was platted in 1859. The city was named after Alton, Illinois. A post office has been in operation in Alton since 1860. Alton was incorporated as a city in 1929. According to the United States Census Bureau, the city has a total area of 1.59 square miles, of which 1.57 square miles is land and 0.02 square miles is water.

The courthouse stands in the center of the square. On the grounds around the square, the Greer Spring Mill stone is on display. Native stones for building the mill were taken from along the Mill Stone Branch of the Warm Fork. Could it be that this stone originated on the Mill Stone Branch?

East of Alton, Bat Cave Hollow is located along Missouri Route FF. in Johnson Township. The area drains into Eleven Points River about three miles north of Riverton. It was named for the cave, which has been for years the habitat of bats. During the Civil War, saltpeter was made here from the "drippings" of the cave.

Bellah Falls was an old crossing on Eleven Points River northeast of Greer Spring. An early family of the name lived nearby. Bellah's Falls was on Eleven Points River between the mouth of Greer Spring Branch and the bridge of Highway 19. The rapids caused a noise resembling that of old-time bellows. Some locals insist on spelling the falls "Bellows," but others give the real origin, the same as that of the crossing.

Cave Springs is located about four miles southeast of Alton are two small caves; one is dry and from the other flows small springs. During the Civil War Major George Norman and William Johnson and two older men, took Joseph Johnson, then a youth, with them when they took the county records to the cave for concealment during the danger. Near the springs was built the old log house for school and church, the Cave Springs.

A different account of this story said that these county records were hidden in Piney Cave near where the old Piney School in Jobe Township had been. No matter the exact location, Major Norman, John C. Johnson, William C. Livingston, Andrew J. Livingston, and others participated in this incident.

Religious services have always been a part of Alton's culture and churches are plentiful around the town. Macedonia Baptist Church was a Missionary Baptist Church located five miles north of Alton. For years, it was also known locally as Elm Pond Church for Elm Pond nearby. The report of the General Association of 1934 gives the organization date as 1902, but elderly residents in 1945 said it is much older.

Shiloh Church was an old, originally log, church located four miles southwest of Alton. It was thought to have been built as early as 1867 or earlier. The church had been used by most of the earlier community which were primarily Baptists and Methodists. The building had also been used for school. A more recent church building was erected in 1921, is a Missionary Baptist, but it was open to other denominations as well. The minutes give the organization date as 1888. Shiloh School, a one-quarter mile away, took the name of the old church. Shiloh Cemetery was earlier known as Crews Cemetery for John Crews who owned the land.

On the first weekend in October every year, Alton has the Walnut Festival where locals and visitors alike enjoy the music and various types of vendors in the area.

KOSHKONONG

On the far western side of Oregon County along Missouri Highway 63, and toward the south is the city of Koshkonong. In the 2020 census, the population was 196. The town was laid out in 1882, taking its name from Lake Koshkonong, in Wisconsin. A post office called Koshkonong has been in operation since 1893.

The small town was established next to the Frisco Railroad. It was established in 1882 by real estate men, including Colonel Dobizie, who served in the Northern Army during the Civil War. Mr. Diggings, the railroad superintendent, suggested that they name the community after Lake Koshkonong in southern Wisconsin, where he enjoyed hunting duck.

A creek and town in Rock County, Wisconsin, bore this name. Koshkonong was an Indian word, and its meaning was not known. Some believe that the word refers to "koshkosh" a word meaning "hog". Others have suggested such meanings as "wild rice," which grew around the Wisconsin lake, or "cross," referring to an Indian village where old trails crossed, or "big water," referring to the lake. It is probably connected with the name Kaskaskia, an Indian word of unknown meaning, the designation of a tribe of Illinois Indians. Of course, the original signification of the name of the lake in Wisconsin doesn't have any connection to the Missouri village, which merely borrowed the name.

According to the United States Census Bureau, the city has a total area of 0.18 square miles.

North of Koshkonong was the Big Apple School. This school was situated in the fruit district where apples were grown abundantly during the early 1900s.

St. Elmo, a discontinued railroad station, was located one and a half miles south of Koshkonong, the shipping point for the St. Elmo Peach and Apple Orchards, a 400-acre peach orchard set in 1898. The orchard was probably named, by Mrs. McNair (wife of Orthwein McNair, one of the promoters) who was a great literary reader. St. Elmo, written in 1866, by Jane Evans Wilson, was widely read. Since a railroad accident is one of the central incidents of the story, it would seem appropriate for a railroad town.

John G. McNair, a grandson of the former Missouri governor, and brother of Orthwein, was the president of the McNair Orchard Company of Kansas City. Their orchard enterprise began in the vicinity of Koshkonong and Thayer in 1893 with 160 acres, mainly apples and peaches. By 1898 there were 3,500 acres. After a few years of flourishing business, the orchards gradually went to ruins.

MYRTLE

Myrtle lies 14 miles southeast of Alton, 14 mi east of Thayer, and approximately three-quarters of a mile north of the Arkansas state line. The community lies on a low ridge above the south side of Mill Creek along Missouri Route V. The town was laid out in 1878 by Scott Moore and named after his daughter Myrtle Moore. The post office in Myrtle has been in operation since 1884.

Stubblefield Ford was an old crossing of Eleven Points River about two miles north of the state line. Clinton and William Stubblefield of Tennessee settled in the vicinity before the Civil War. Stubblefield Graveyard is no longer used. Stubblefield Creek, another name for Colvin Creek enters Eleven Points River near the Ford and took the name of the pioneer settlers. By 1916 the river had become deeper at the ford and a ferry was put in, known as Huddleston Ferry because it was first operated by Lon Huddleston. A bridge now spans the river.

Several grist mills had been operated along the stream near Myrtle at various times. Some owners and operators at various times were James Young, Joe Stubblefield, John Taylor, and Hiram Kirk.

Today, the children of Myrtle attend Couch Public School which lies approximately three miles northwest of town along Missouri Highway 142.

Every autumn on the last Saturday in September, Myrtle has a festival called Myrtle Yester-Daze where locals get together to celebrate their community.

ROVER

Rover lies approximately eleven miles west of Alton. Take P Highway to Missouri Route M turn right, and the town is, 1.5 miles south of U.S. Route 160. Nathaniel Haywood established the first store and blacksmith shop in Rover.

He became the first postmaster and cared for the mail from his store. The name for Rover was established after Rab Jolliff suggested naming the town after Mr. Haywood's dog Rover. The post office was established in 1900 and remained in operation until 1945.

Jolliff Cemetery is located about two miles northeast of Rover. During the Civil War, there was a little skirmish near the Jolliff home, and Captain Maples was sent to suppress the bushwhackers. He was killed and buried there. After the war, Randall C. Jolliff, who had come from Illinois during the 1850s, deeded the land for a church and cemetery. The Shiloh Hardshell Baptist Church was generally known as Jolliff Church. The church only had a Baptist minister for a short time. The old log house was also used for school. The school was later torn down and used when they built a new school which took the name of the church and leader Jolliff.

THOMASVILLE

Thomasville is located nine miles northwest of Alton just off State Highway 160 on Route 99. It rests the river hollows east of West Plains and was once the center of civilization on a wild American frontier.

Samuel Hatcher settled near the present site of Thomasville in 1816. However, some claim that the first settlement was made here by Charles Hatcher in 1803.

Another account says that in 1812, a party of six men traveled from Slaughterville, Kentucky by way of the land office in Jackson, Cape Girardeau, Missouri. They rode across several steams and numerous swamps into a settlement of Osage Indians in the Eleven Point River Valley.

They decided to set up camp there and homestead. About four years later, according to old newspapers, another party of from six to eight families arrived, and the first white settlement In the Ozarks took root.

The earliest settlers in the Thomasville area called it Rich Woods. It is the oldest settlement in the county and adjacent region. The country was rich in land, timber, and wild animals. Rich Hill was the name given to his home, three miles north of Thomasville, Charles Hatcher, a Revolutionary soldier, who settled there in 1809.

The original county seat of Oregon County was laid out in 1846, incorporated in 1873, and named by the County Court after George Thomas who settled one mile north of Thomasville on land that was later owned by Charles Gum.

The Thomas family had come to the area in 1817. George Thomas had four sons: Lee, Julian, Marshall, and Stonewall Jackson, and two daughters: Lydia and Jane. They became heads of prominent families. In 1818 the Bellah, Huddleston, and Howell families came.

The village was the center of commerce for a time. West Plains in Howell County took its name from being on the plains west of Thomasville.

The 1850 map shows this to be a settlement or village on Eleven Points River at the crossing of the old roads extending north, northeast, south, southeast, and southwest. It was later known as Thomasville.

Thomasville was platted in 1846 and was the original county seat. The community was named for George Thomas, a pioneer settler. A post office called Thomasville was established in 1846 and remained in operation until 1979.

Mint Spring School was three miles southwest of Thomasville, near a good spring where the mint plant grew abundantly. The original school, a log house, known as McKelvey School was on land belonging to William McKelvey, three miles north of the school site. When the school was moved, in the early 1890s, for a good water supply, the school's name was changed, discontinued, and consolidated with Thomasville. Because of deterioration, Thomasville school was incorporated with Alton in 1991.

Middle Fork is the branch of Eleven Points River, that flows through Thomasville. Like most of the Eleven Point, it is fed by springs.

North Prong and South Prong of the Eleven Point converge two and a half miles south of Thomasville to make Barren Fork. The name was suggested. It offered a good grazing region because it was barren of timber during the pioneer days.

On the South Prong of Barren Fork. Josiah Howell had a sawmill in the early 1880s. West Prong and East Prong converge to form Mill Creek.

Old's Mill was a water grist mill, one mile south of Thomasville on Eleven Points River. It was established during the 1850s by Thomas Old, an early settler and landowner, who came from Virginia to Oregon County in 1841 and settled at Thomasville. It was burned during the Civil War. The early burial ground, Old's Cemetery was one-quarter mile south of Thomasville and has not been used for at least one hundred years

They established a trading post and a land office. From there they could travel back to Jackson to trade furs for salt, coffee, and lead. The trip of 150 miles each way could only be covered by canoeing on the river.

They made their homemade gunpowder from sumac charcoal and saltpeter mined from a cave upriver from Thomasville.

By the mid-1830s, the Osage were driven west into Oklahoma Territory. Thomasville continued to grow and thrive, and other settlements began branching out. By the 1850s, one such town had taken root on the fertile prairies west of Thomasville, on the 'west plains."

In 1882, the Kansas City, Fort Scott, and Memphis Railroad sent its route along the high ground through West Plains. The river bottoms proved too soft for the iron track. Again in 1887, Thomasville was bypassed when the Current River Railroad branched away east, scattering the little new towns of Willow Springs, Mountain View, Birch Tree, and Montier in its wake.

River travel had lost to the railroads as the primary transportation method across the frontier. At the same time, Missouri counties were redrawn and reapportioned. Thomasville, once the center of Oregon County lost its status as the county seat of Oregon County to Alton.

Thomasville, lying in its fertile valley, was attached to the world only by unimproved wagon roads, and instead of the center of civilization, had become only a central hamlet for area farmers and frontiersmen for whom the frontier had moved on.

The American economy fluctuated wildly between boom and bust and boom again, and towns that could not adapt to a changing population pattern were dying off. However, Thomasville just kept on living on a much smaller scale. Although it no longer grew, the town still held its own.

At the beginning of the twentieth century, progress came to town in the form of a steam engine for threshing wheat. An electrical generator provided lights for downtown Thomasville, long before the Rural Electrification Association came with its poles and strands of power to connect Thomasville with the world.

For years, Thomasville went on much the same as the rest of the world changed. The road from Thomasville to West Plains became a highway and was paved by the state. What had been a two-day trip by wagon could be done in a single morning by car. Local stores began to carry once-rare supplies. Families that had once ordered salt in 250-lb. barrels from St. Louis, shipped by train to Mtn. View and by wagon to Thomasville, used the telephone to place their orders with a local grocer and began buying what they needed for the next week, instead of for the next year.

In Thomasville, there still exists the spirit of the Ozarks of the frontier, of the Osage, a curiously timeless place that hangs suspended as the world passes from age to age. Over the years the town has become a sleepy version of itself. Thomasville School was built in 1930 and in 1991 became a community building. The school-children now traveled to Alton for their education.

High Wassie and Low Wassie

Low Wassie Creek was a small eastern branch of Spring Creek. The lower part of the valley was formerly known as Low Wassie Hollow, and the upper part as High Wassie Hollow. Through the valley ran the old road from Thomasville to Piedmont in Wayne County. Presumably located in the two parts of the valley respectively are the post offices listed by Campbell in 1874. High Wassie was a post office ten miles north of Alton. Low Wassie was a post office thirteen miles northeast of Alton. Low Wassie appeared on the postal lists of 1862 and 1867, but neither of them appeared among Oregon County post offices in later postal guides, or on later maps of the county. One of the two places must be identical with the "Yowassie" placed in the northeast corner of the county on Colton's Sectional Map of Missouri of 1867. This should not be confused with the town in Shannon County called Low Wassie, located on Pike Creek. Today, the two hollows also have lost their old names. High Wassie Hollow became known as Three Mile Spring Hollow, for its spring on the old Thomasville-Piedmont Road, a famous place for early travelers and teamsters to make camp. Low Wassie Hollow, and likewise Low Wassie Creek, became called Two Mile Spring Hollow, for the approximate length of the lower part of the valley.

The origin of the old names is interesting. They appear to be Indian in origin. It seems probable that they are the oldest names of locations in the county. Hiwassee, or its variant Yowassia on the 1867 map, is presumably closest to the original form.

The name Hiwassee is used for the Hiwassee River in Tennessee, and the word was originally Ayuhwasi, meaning "savannah" or "meadow."

Cherokees who relocated to what is now Oregon County in the early part of the 19th century seem to have brought this name with them. Shortly after 1800 numbers of the more conservative Cherokees, wearied by the encroachments of the whites, left their homes in North and South Carolina, Georgia, and Tennessee, and crossed the Mississippi to make new homes in the wilderness in Arkansas and some in parts of southern Missouri including Oregon County although most of this part of the state was inhabited by the Osage.

The names High Wassie to Low Wassie are instances of popular etymology. The name Low Wassie was named because of a sinkhole located close to the village. "Wassie" became a dialectic term for a rain wash or a swamp." The word "wassie" or "wossie" was used locally in the sense of swamp or rain wash. It seems likely that this is an interesting survival in the Ozark dialect of a word or form that has become obsolete in standard English.

The pioneers were merely following the ordinary processes of popular etymology, by replacing an Indian term that was of course unintelligible to them by a familiar dialect word. Out of Hiwassie, interpreted as "High Wassie," they first created "Low Wassie," and then understood "Wassie" as a common noun. The fact that the whole region is amply supplied with small springs, marshy spots, and sinkholes would have given frequent occasions for the use of such a topographical term as "wassie."

THAYER

Thayer is the largest city in Oregon County, on State Highway 63 just north of the Arkansas line. The city has a total area of 2.44 square miles (6.32 km2), all land. The town had been platted on December 2, 1882, by George H. Nettleton of Kansas City, the first president of the Fort Scott, Kansas City, and Memphis Railroad (now Frisco), and named after his wife. When the post office was established, the name had to be changed because there was another Augusta in the state in St. Charles County, which had a post office since 1853 so the town had to be renamed.

Upon a petition of most of the citizens of the town, the circuit court, on August 24, 1886, agreed on the name of Thayer after Nathaniel Thayer of Boston, Massachusetts, a very wealthy stockholder of the railroad company.

Thayer is located very close to the historic route taken by Native Americans during their forced relocation to Oklahoma in the 1830s. This event is known as the Trail of Tears, and it is one of the most tragic episodes in American history.

During the Civil War, this border county in this border state was hard hit by neighbor-against-neighbor bushwhacker fighting. When it was still Augusta, the town played an important role in the Civil War, with both Union and Confederate forces passing through the area. It was the location of a major engagement in 1862 when Union forces under General Samuel R. Curtis defeated a Confederate detachment led by General James McIntosh.

After the war, Thayer became a railroad town when the tracks were laid in 1882. Around the turn of the 20th century, 400 railroad men lived in Thayer.

On August 16, 1904, a train on the Frisco line derailed near Thayer, killing 31 people and injuring dozens more. Currently, the BNSF (Burlington Northern Santa Fe) railroad travels through town.

The area was deeply affected by Prohibition, which began in 1920. The area became a hub for bootlegging and other illegal activities, and many residents were involved in the production and distribution of alcohol.

Even though Thayer is a small town, it played a role in the larger struggle for civil rights in America. In 1955, a group of black residents staged a sit-in at a local diner, demanding equal treatment and access to public spaces.

Barren Hollow leads into Warm Fork just below Clifton. No timber grew there during the pioneer days' because old timers said that you, "Couldn't get enough timber for a riding switch."

Barren Hollow School was a pioneer school in the vicinity of Barren Hollow long before the Civil War. The original old log house one mile east of the site of Clifton School, Methodist and Baptist churches was also used the building for services, When Clifton School was built, the old house was abandoned. During the 1890s, as the population increased. Eventually, the Barren Hollow District formed from parts of Clifton and other districts. Eventually, this school then incorporated into Thayer's school district.

Not far from Thayer was Boise City. This early village was located just across the state line from Mammoth Springs, Arkansas. In truth, it was part of Mammoth Springs on the Missouri side. During the early 1880s, when the railroad was being built, it was a thriving town, with a store and saloon. Its growth was encouraged by the Arkansas alcohol prohibition laws.

The town was founded by a man who came over the state line and helped to get the town incorporated so that he could sell liquor with impunity. The community has since entirely disappeared. When the post office was established, in 1883, Charles Trantham suggested the name Spring City. Trantham was a leading merchant and lifelong resident. Later Spring City was changed to Boise City, which some informants thought was an old family name in the vicinity. Other locals believed the town was named for a man who operated a small grist mill nearby.

Yet another account suggested it was named for Governor Horace Boies of Iowa, but both spelling and dates make this unlikely. Boies served two terms as the state governor, from 1889 to 1893, and became prominent outside of Iowa only in 1896, when he was one of the leading but unsuccessful candidates for the presidential nomination at the Democratic National Convention. The spelling, but not the pronunciation, would suggest that the name was borrowed from Boise City, the capital of Idaho. According to another man, the Idaho city takes its name from the Boise River, a French word meaning "woody," given by the early French traders because of the trees upon the banks of the river. The precise origin remains a mystery.

UNINCORPORATED
COMMUNITIES

If you look around Oregon County, you'll see green signs placed throughout the county indicating communities that no longer exist or have little more than a couple of houses remaining.

Bardley One such location is Bardley which is an unincorporated community on the Oregon/Ripley County line. It is located on Missouri Route J approximately two miles north of U.S. Route 160 and fourteen miles east of Alton.

Bardley started as a logging town in 1895. The community was named after Bordley, Kentucky, the native home of the first settler. The difference in the names occurred when the post office misspelled Bordley which was never corrected. A post office called Bardley was established in 1895 and remained in operation until 1966.

Billmore is an unincorporated community in southeastern Oregon County located on Highway 142 in the Mark Twain National Forest approximately 17 miles east of Thayer. The community takes its name from Billmore Hollow, the valley in which it is located.

Soon after the Civil War William Moore, known as Bill Moore (or More), settled in the valley away from other settlements. As settlers came a post office was established in 1885 and remained in operation until 1906. The small village grew up but soon disappeared including the school that was situated three and a half miles northeast of Myrtle.

Braswell A post office called Braswell was established in 1894 and remained in operation until 1915. The community has the name of Thomas Braswell, a first settler. Rural routes made it unnecessary,

Thomas Braswell, whose father John Lemuel Baswell came from Tennessee in 1856 and settled there, was a landowner and teacher in the county for several years. He later served as a state representative in the early 1890s for the Republicans. Braswell Tower was located there.

Calm In southeastern Oregon County lies the unincorporated community of Calm. The community is located at the junction of Missouri routes 142 and UU, one mile east of the Eleven Point River and two miles west of the Oregon/ Ripley County line.

A post office called Calm was established in 1898 and remained in operation until 1907. The local tradition of the origin of the name occurred when the citizens were discussing what to name their settlement and several names were suggested. John Miller's daughter, who had been to Salem, Massachusetts had recently come in on the mail cart. To her, all was so quiet in this rural section, and she suggested they name the village Calm.

Clifton The post office and village were established about two miles northeast of Thayer, on what was then the old Thomasville and Salem, Arkansas road. Established before 1874, Clifton became a little village with a population of 300. They built a building in 1880 to use as a church, school, and the Masonic lodge. Its name, the "town of Cliffs," originated from two prominent landowners and merchants, George and William J. Cliff, who settled there soon after the Civil War. When the railroad was built, the population of this village gradually moved to Thayer.

The Palmer Graveyard was a very old burial ground one and a half miles north of Clifton. An early pioneer of that name had lived there.

Coin A village named Coin was in Bat Cave Hollow along what is now Missouri Route FF. A post office was established in 1895 and remained in operation until 1909. The community was named after Coin Jones, an early settler.

Coin Jones, came with his father, George Jones, from Kansas in about 1894. A sawmill, a grist mill, and a store were set up on the settlement and soon a post office was established. Coin Jones ran it. The post office closed when mail delivery was established in the area.

Corona A post office called Corona was established in 1900 and remained in operation until 1906. Porter Arnold suggested the name probably because of the coppery or golden color of the spring water.

Couch is a small, unincorporated community in Oregon County, Missouri, United States. It is located six miles south of Alton on Missouri Route A. The post office of Couch was established in 1887 and is still in operation. The community got its name from George W. Couch, one of the first settlers in the county, who lived on the old Simpson Couch homestead. He was an influential citizen and landowner. He owned and operated a cotton gin, store, and corn mill there.

An earlier Couch mill was owned by William Williams. Born in Scotland, Williams bought the mill before or around 1867. The dam washed out, and he sold it in the early 1870s to the Hardin Brothers bought it and tried to keep the dam repaired. However, they soon gave up and the old mill went to ruins.

Deckard Another community called Deckard was named after Kellis Deckard, a local tradesman. Kellis Deckard, farmer, and land-owner, owned a blacksmith shop. His grandfather, James Deckard, had a blacksmith shop here fifty years ago.

Farewell is a community on Missouri Route V approximately eight miles east of Thayer. It is one-half mile north of the Missouri-Arkansas state line. The community of Jeff is 1.5 miles to the west on Route V and Myrtle is five miles to the east.

Farewell had been a small timber village. The post office was established in 1912 and remained in operation until 1927. J.W. Linebarger first kept the post office in his home. It was moved from Jeff in 1913. One reason given for the town's name was that the postal department refused to give it the name "Fairview. However, another suggestion for the name was because Mr. James H. Taylor had been the only postmaster at Jeff and this was a farewell to him.

Garfield is an unincorporated community in southeast Oregon County and is located along Missouri Route E, approximately three miles southeast of Couch. Garfield's post office was established in 1882 and remained in operation until 1906. The community was named after James A. Garfield, the 20th President of the United States. The village had earlier been known as Sittonville after a captain of the Confederate Army, John J. Sitton, who kept a store on his farm. When the post office was established in his store, Thomas Hays, an old army chum of his, suggested the name for President James A. Garfield (1831-1881), who had been assassinated a few years earlier.

A community building was built for all denominations near the site of the old post office of Garfield. Originally it was a Method-ist Church supported chiefly by John L. Sitton, whose wife "Aunt

Nannie," was very religious. It was a small building, but neat and painted white. As it was unusual for rural schools and churches to be painted, it was generally known as White Church.

Griswold was in the southeast corner of the county. Griswold's post office was established in 1887 and closed in 1907. The community was named after James Griswold, a local merchant.

James Griswold had a store, a cotton gin, a grist mill, and a post office but all were gone before 1910. It is said that a drunken man killed a member of a wedding party in the village one evening, and people began moving away after the incident.

Guiteau started as a country store named after presidential assassin Charles J. Guiteau, and the town was intended to rival nearby Garfield. Besides the store, the community had a church and a schoolhouse.

As the story goes, soon after the assassination of President Garfield in 1881, Robert Hall set up a store about three miles southeast of Garfield saying that he would kill that village. Since the Sitton store was spoken of as Garfield, this store became known as Guiteau, after Charles J. Guiteau, President Garfield's assassin. While some political enmity remained in the community, when the Garfield District was divided, the new school, Guiteau, took the name of the Hall Store. The store failed to develop into a village and soon the proprietor moved to Oklahoma.

Hollis was an old community named for the local Hollis family. The family were pioneer settlers of Oregon County. The settlement was also known as "East Tennessee" because it was the most eastern settlement of Tennessee at that time." The Livingston family and others had come from the same state.

Huddleston A post office called Huddleston was established in 1855 and remained in operation until 1860. John Huddleston settled in the county before the Civil War and the community was named after Benjamin Huddleston, an early pioneer.

Jeff was a community on Missouri Highway V approximately seven miles east of Thayer. It is one mile north of the Missouri-Arkansas state line. The community of Farewell is 1.5 miles to the east on Route V.

Jeff's post office was established in 1884. In 1883, Mr. James H. Taylor, former postmaster and merchant, applied to establish a post office on the old star route from Gatewood to Mammoth Springs. He offered "Jeffers" for Joseph Jeffers, a Cherokee Indian who owned land and operated the grist mill nearby, but the postal authorities, afraid of confusion, kept the first part of the name only. The post office closed in 1914. For several years afterward, only the store remained of the little village.

Jobe The town was pronounced by locals as Jo-bee and is a variant of the name Job. In 1830, Eli Job came from Tennessee with his family when his son Jacob was five years of age. He purchased the land. A post office called "Jobe" was established in 1848 and closed in 1888. The post reopened under the spelling "Job" in 1892 and closed in 1906. The post office was permanently closed in 1907 when a mail route was established coming from Couch.

Jobe was in southeastern Oregon County. approximately seven miles east of Couch and five and one-half miles north of the Missouri-Arkansas border. Frederick Creek flows past the north side of the community and the Eleven Point River is three and a half miles to the east.

It had once been described as a "thriving little village twenty-one miles southeast of Alton." Later maps and postal guides gave the spelling "Job" which was the true spelling for the family who first owned the land. Jacob Job had been a landowner and influential citizen there. In 1945, Mr. William L. Gum owned the Job land and operated a large stock farm there.

Lulu (also called Lula) is on the Mark Twain National Forest boundary along county Road 129 approximately one mile north of U.S. Route 160 and five miles east of Alton. A small church by the same name is still attended by parishioners in the area.

Lula's post office was established in 1908 and closed in 1915. An unnamed Baptist minister had suggested that the community be named after William J. Stairs' wife Lula. Stairs was a landowner and former judge of the county.

Many Springs (pronounced locally as Manny Springs) had a post office established in 1875 that closed in 1907. The community was named this because of the many springs near the original town site.

A village and post office was about nine miles southeast of Alton just off what is now Missouri Highway 160. In the early days, mail was brought by horseback from Doniphan. Now the mail to the community comes on a rural route from Alton. Sadly, like many of these communities, this one is all but deserted now.

Midway was named because it's located midway between Alton and Thayer. There was a store, filling station, and blacksmith shop. In 1907 Geo. W. Moore, from Indiana, built a neighborhood blacksmith shop, known as Moore's Shop. The store was added in 1914.

If you pay attention as you're going down Missouri Highway 19 toward Thayer, on the left, you'll see the remnants of a filling station on the left-hand side of the highway.

Mitch was a discontinued post office one and a half miles northeast of Riverton. The post office was kept by George Kellums, a farmer, in his home. The name was a shortened form for Norman A. Mitchell, who was a leading farmer and landowner of the community.

Mitchell School had been one of the older schools in the area. It was named for Norman A. Mitchell, an influential farmer and landowner in the community. Later, as the result of a local squabble, the district was divided into Districts No. 37 and No. 38. District No. 37 was still known as Mitchell School, but was given the name Seed Tick, because those insects so common on the hills, was a term of derision.

New Liberty An early post office near the site of New Liberty was called Butts. This original name took the name of an early settler, John Butts, who owned a store and operated an over-shot wheel grist mill during the late 1870s and early 1880s. For several years before he died in 1889, he served as justice of the peace and postmaster.

At this time the post office was discontinued until 1901, when James Brawley, a farmer and landowner, took charge of the mail in his home. The office bore his name until 1915 when he turned it over to his son-in-law, L. Allman, who changed the village's name to New Liberty after the nearby school.

New Liberty's post office remained in operation from 1914-1941. In addition to the post office, the village had a schoolhouse.

Pinkleyville An old village and post office two miles south of Garfield on the old Alton to Pocahontas road. Emanuel Pinkley had a blacksmith shop there on his farm. Later a store and post office were established. His sons, Jeff and Ed, owned land nearby. The place was also known locally as Scott Town because Green Scott owned a store and post office.

Ross A post office was established in Ross in 1914, Samuel Ross kept a post office in his home. The post office was discontinued after two or three months, and the mail was handled out of Greer.

A large spring marked the homeplace of Samuel Ross who came from Tennessee in 1866. A school, near Big Hurricane, was named for him. The cemetery of the same name, on the Ross farm, became a public burial ground but had begun as a family graveyard. The Ross Ford of Eleven Points River was the crossing of the old Alton-Van Buren Road.

Royal Oak can be found on U.S. Route 160, between Alton and Thomasville approximately five miles northwest of Alton. Dry Creek flows past approximately one-half mile east of the location.

A post office called Royal Oak was established in 1894 and remained in operation until 1895. In addition to the post office, Royal Oak had a church, a store, and a school. The site was named Royal Oak because of a nearby tract of oak trees.

The old school, located about seven miles northwest of Alton had been built in a grove of oak trees. The oak is considered the king of trees; hence the "Royal" part of the title. The store (the building of which can still be seen but has fallen in disrepair) on Highway 19, one and a half miles southeast took the name of the school. The store was established by Emory Uzzle in the early 1890s but was operated by some other persons at various times.

It was later known as Crews Store also, for W.E. Crews who made considerable improvements and owned it for about ten years. He sold the store to E.N. Wallace in 1937. The old blacksmith shop and shack for the early store had been replaced by a more modern building for a filling station, store, and bus station for the Golden Arrow Bus Line from Thayer to St. Louis. The place is still known as the Royal Oak Store.

The service station and grocery store in 1937 were owned and operated by Ernest Wallace. The Wallace family eventually joined with the Owens family and started the Wallace and Owens Grocery chain and sold the property in Royal Oak. The grocery store chain grew to eight grocery stores before it was sold to Harps Food Stores on November 12, 2008.

Webster An old post office and trading post of some importance six miles south of Alton. Lemuel Braswell, who came from Tennessee in 1856, got the office established and kept it in a store. One report said that it was established in 1869, but another lists it as a post office in 1862. The village was named for Noah Webster (1758-1843), the famous lexicographer.

Wilderness is found at the end of Missouri Route K within the Irish Wilderness area of the Mark Twain National Forest. The Eleven Point River is three miles to the southeast and Alton is twelve miles to the southeast. A post office called Wilderness was established in 1882 and remained in operation until 1954.

The community derives its name from the old Irish Wilderness Settlement that was abandoned during the violence of the Civil War. Robert A. King, a Presbyterian minister, was the first postmaster in 1881.

Woodside was located on Missouri Route 19 approximately three miles north of Alton. A post office called Woodside was established in 1856, and continued operations until 1916. The community was named after J. R. Woodside, another early pioneer.

OTHER PLACES OF INTEREST IN OREGON COUNTY

THE IRISH WILDERNESS

An early settlement, primarily located in Ripley County, a few miles north of the present site of Bardley was sponsored by Reverend John Hogan, priest of St. Michael's Parish of St. Louis. Father Hogan and others, imbued with the "missionary spirit", soon after the panic of 1857, set about to aid the poor Irish, good home and peace-loving Catholics, many of whom were distressed railroad laborers. Some had fled from persecution in Ireland. Reverend James Fox, of Old Mines, Missouri, bought a tract of land for the settlement. A one-story long house, 40 ft. square, was erected, and partitioned; one, for a chapel. The other was for the private residence. They cleared land, built homes, and dug wells. By the spring of 1859, about forty families had settled on land they purchased at twelve and a half cents an acre, or on improved farms nearby. Father Hogan himself arrived in November 1858.

The settlement's western border was the Eleven Point River in Oregon County, It extended east past the Current River in Ripley County, and as far east as Doniphan, Missouri. Some land in Oregon and neighboring Ripley County was bought and donated by Reverend James Fox. In 1859 about forty families settled in the wilderness, and more were on their way.

The settlement was populated between 1859 through 1863. During the Civil War, marauding bands devastated the settlement. Some were killed; all who could flee to other states or sections. The region, in ruins and covered with much timber, was later known as the Irish Wilderness. Some land was sold for taxes. The timber was removed by the Ozark, Land and Lumber Company and the Moss Tie Company.

The roads that crossed straight through the heart of the settlement, including the Old Bellevue (or Bellview) Road, made the settlers vulnerable to Union and Confederate troops, murderers, and criminals. By the end of 1863, the settlement had been destroyed, and all settlers had fled or died. Union Major James Wilson contributed to the destruction of the settlement.

William Hatfield later owned the Old Priest Field about two miles southeast of Wilderness. It was recorded that as late as the mid-1940s the area was grown in timber. The ruins of the well, a pile of stones that made the foundation, and a few descendants of the early settlers remained to mark the missionary efforts.

Today, the Irish Wilderness is a 16,227-acre wilderness area in Missouri located in the far northeastern corner of Oregon County. This area is separated from the rest of the county by the Eleven Point River. In 1984, the U.S. Congress designated it a wilderness. The Irish Wilderness is located within the Eleven Point Ranger District of the Mark Twain National Forest, 10 miles northeast of Alton, Missouri. It is one of eight wilderness areas protected and preserved in Missouri.

Within the Mark Twain National Forest, the Irish Wilderness is the largest federally protected wilderness area in the state. Hiking, backpacking, and horseback riding opportunities abound on the Ozark Trail and the White's Creek Trail. Canoeing, kayaking, boating, and fishing are popular on the Eleven Point River, Missouri's only National Wild and Scenic River.

Hiking and horseback riding are popular on the White's Creek Trail, an 18.6-mile trail throughout the wilderness. Attractions include White's Creek Cave (temporarily gated to protect endangered bats), Fiddler and Bliss Springs, traces of old tramway railroads, and overlooks of the Eleven Point River. The karst topography of the area creates very scenic views along this trail. Wildlife seen in the wilderness area include black bears, mountain lions, whitetail deer, timber rattlesnakes, turkeys, and bald eagles.

GREER SPRING RECREATION AREA

Greer Spring, previously known by some as Big Ozark Spring, is the second largest natural spring in Missouri. It is one of the largest springs in the United States and lies twelve miles northeast of Alton. Its average flow of 209,000,000 gallons rushes from under a precipitous bluff, a most picturesque surrounding, and flows with a fall of 46 ft. through a narrow, rocky gorge with heavily wooded slopes to Eleven Points River, one and a half miles away. Greer Spring is one of the scenic gems of the Ozarks, It is a place of unusual beauty and grandeur.

The spring flows for over a mile before emptying into Eleven Point River. Greer Spring water comes from sinkholes and nearby streams that flow underground. It supports a diverse number of aquatic invertebrates, including some endangered species.

A community had once been at Greer. The post office at Greer was established on January 10, 1890, and closed in 1941. The community was named after Samuel Greer, a Civil War veteran, and pioneer.

Its first postmaster, Mr. Peter Williams, was still serving in 1937. He suggested the name for the post office be in memory of Captain Samuel Greer of the Confederate army, who had owned the land before the Civil War. The post office was discontinued between 1939-1941.

Greer lies on Missouri Route 19 between Alton to the south-southwest and Winona to the north. Route 19 crosses the Eleven

Point River at Greer Crossing, approximately three miles northeast of where the village had been. Greer Spring lies just to the north of the river access.

A large three-story flour mill, built in 1888 upon the hill about one-quarter mile from Greer Spring. It was run by a cable from the large water well at the spring. Because of competition, it has not been in operation since 1916. The original small grist mill set in the spring of 1855 was known as the Simpson Mill after its owner Thomas C. Simpson, a pioneer Baptist minister from Tennessee, who sold it to Captain Samuel Greer during the Civil War.

An old and large burial ground called Simpson Graveyard was two and a half miles south of Greer. The graveyard was started on land owned by Thomas C. Simpson, a Baptist minister and pioneer, who came from Tennessee in 1853. He represented the county in the Legislature in 1858 and during the 1880s served as judge of the county. The cemetery is now Bailey Cemetery. Daniel Bailey, who came from Tennessee in 1858, purchased land nearby. His son, Harvey Bailey, father deeded more land for the cemetery and changed the name.

The Greer millstone is currently on display on the grounds around the Oregon County Courthouse on the Square in Alton.

A defunct church, Bethany Baptist, was organized in 1900 by Reverend Joe Glass of Kentucky. The building, located one-quarter mile east of the Greer post office, was bought by the Greer School District and used for the public school for many years.

Today, on the north side of where the bridge at Greer crosses the river, you'll find the Greer Spring River Access where you can put in a kayak or canoe if you would like. Near the river access are the campgrounds. For a nominal fee, you can set up tent camping there.

Travel south on Missouri State Highway 19, you'll see the old rebuilt mill building. There's still work that needs to be done to make it explorable, but you can look around the outside of the building. Greer Mill was listed on the National Register of Historic Places in 2005.

South of the river access on Missouri Highway 19, is the trail that leads to the actual spring of Greer Spring. Greer Spring trail is nine-tenths of a mile-long walking trail that goes down to the actual spring itself. It's a bit steep, but the trail is beautiful.

The trailhead should be easy to find once you pull into the parking lot. According to the USDA Forest Service, the trail leads hikers past a variety of trees such as oak, shortleaf pine, hickory, flowering dogwoods, and sassafras.

FALLING SPRINGS

Falling Spring is another natural spring located in Missouri's Mark Twain National Forest. This spring gets its name from the small waterfall that forms from spring waters pouring from a rock into a small pond.

Falling Spring once powered two mills, one of which remains standing to this day. Falling Spring Mill was built using timber between 1927 and 1929 and later enclosed with rough lumber siding. It was used for grinding corn for feed, sawing out shingles and firewood, and later generating electricity.

Today you can visit the remains of Falling Spring Mill. On the site, the remains of Tomas Brown Cabin, the first of four houses built near the spring, can still be seen. A rustic picnic area lies beside the spring.

Like Greer Spring, Falling Spring lies within Mark Twain National Forest in Oregon County. To reach Falling springs from Alton, go north on Missouri Highway 19. Falling Spring is located off the highway to the left on County Road 3164. After traveling a couple of miles on a gravel road you will pass the Falling Spring Cemetery and come across the parking lot for Falling Spring Mill.

MCCORMACK LAKE

From Winona, go south on Highway 19 for 12-13 miles, then take a right into McCormack Lake Road (FS 4155). The trail begins near the dam. Travel this road (drivable for any vehicle) for two miles to the lake.

From Alton travel North on Missouri Highway 19 approximately 13.1 miles. Look for the entrance sign on your left, approx. four miles past the Eleven Point River bridge.

A trailhead in the McCormack Lake Day Use Area offers hiking for the 1.07-mile McCormack Lake spur, which connects to the Eleven Point Section of the Ozark Trail and the Lazy C Trail.

The 15-acre lake, surrounded by maple trees is annually stocked with pan fish and bass. During warm months, however, the vegetation makes fishing and boating difficult. The lake does not allow motorboats. However, the use of trolling motors is permitted.

Fishing and Boating - The 15-acre lake is stocked annually with panfish and bass being the catch of the day. During the warm months, the vegetation in the lake can make fishing and boating difficult. The lake is a non-motorized area; boat motors are not allowed. An electric trolling motor is permitted. There is ample parking for picnickers and fishermen.

The area offers limited picnic tables, fire rings, and lantern posts. A vault toilet is provided, but no water is offered on this site.

WHERE THE BEATLES VISITED OREGON COUNTY.

The ranch where the Beatles spent about 72 hours one weekend was named many things over the years, but I am going to call it Pigman Ranch because that was the ranch's name when the Beatles visited the ranch in 1964.

R.M. Hitt, a fruit agent of Koshkonong, and his brother John Hitt of Chicago bought the Boyd Ranch and other land at the close of World War I. The Boyd Ranch was started about 1910. In 1933 it was sold to Dr. J.D. Brock of Kansas City.

What is today often referred to as the Pigman Ranch, Brock Ranch was a large ranch of about 10,000 acres, owned by J.D. Brock, an eye specialist and aviator of Kansas City. It includes the Hitt and Boyd ranches and the old Sitton and Cal. Smith places on Eleven Points River. On the ranch, he has a good clubhouse and a small aviation field. It was later purchased by a man named Pigman.

On September 19, 1964, the locals became excited when they discovered that the Beatles were spending a few days at what then was called the Pigman Ranch. The owner, Reed Pigman, flew the members of the Beatles for a 72-hour rest on his private plane to his private airstrip. The only one not to fly into the ranch was Paul McCartney who drove a pickup truck up from Arkansas.

Pigman Ranch is the only place in America where the Beatles band stopped for some rest and relaxation on their 1964 USA Tour.

That wasn't the end of the drama surrounding that ranch. In 2016 then Democratic Governor Jay Nixon announced that the state had purchased the ranch to create an Eleven Point State Park which never opened.

A lawsuit was filed that argued that 625 of the land was within the federal easement along the river which restricted the property for agricultural purposes only.

GRAND GULF STATE PARK

Grand Gulf State Park is a state-operated, privately owned, and publicly accessible, geologic preserve near Thayer in southern Oregon County. This gulf encompasses a forked canyon that is the remains of an ancient collapsed dolomite cave system. The parkland was acquired by Conservationist Leo Drey (1917–2015) acquired the land before the property was included in the Missouri State Parks System. This 322-acre state park has been operated by the Missouri Department of Natural Resources under a lease agreement with the L-A-D Foundation since 1984. Grand Gulf was declared a National Natural Landmark in 1971 because it is an excellent example of karst topography and underground stream piracy. A 60-acre portion of the park was designated as Grand Gulf Natural Area in 1986.

Some people call Grand Gulf State Park the "Little Grand Canyon." Others simply call it "breathtaking." The park presents the most spectacular collapsed cave system in the Ozarks.

Grand Gulf is nearly one mile long and up to 130 feet deep with steep sides. The part of the original cavern section of the original cavern roof that had not collapsed spans 250 feet. It is one of the largest natural bridges in Missouri. A watershed of 28 square miles feeds into the gulf which drains into a cave entrance at its eastern end. Dye traces proved that the water exiting Grand Gulf feeds into Mammoth Spring in Arkansas, nine miles away.

Visitors can view the gulf from trails on top or from the floor of the canyon where they can walk under the natural bridge, which spans 250 feet with a 75-foot-high opening. There is no official trail leading to the bottom, so visitors should use extreme caution if they attempt to access the bottom.

The park has picnicking facilities and two trails from which to view the gulf. Heavy foliage during the spring and summer makes fall and winter the best seasons to view the canyon.

MAMMOTH SPRING STATE PARK

An honorable mention when visiting Oregon County is that you shouldn't miss when visiting the area just across the Missouri/Arkansas state line in Mammoth Spring, Arkansas. Mammoth Spring State Park is a 62.5-acre Arkansas State Park in Fulton County, Arkansas right on Highway 63.

The Spring

Mammoth Spring originates in the park and averages a flow rate of 9,780,000 US gallons of water per hour at a cool 58 degrees Fahrenheit. As stated earlier, in the section about Grand Gulf State Park, rainfall in southern Missouri percolates into the ground, flows through Grand Gulf State Park, and reemerges as Mammoth Spring in Arkansas.

Mammoth Spring is the largest spring in Arkansas and the third largest in the Ozarks.

The Park

The park surrounding the landmark offers fishing, boating, and hiking in addition to an Arkansas Welcome Center and a restored 1886 St. Louis–San Francisco Railway (Frisco) depot operating as a railroad museum. The site became a state park in 1957, but the park continued to add area until 1975.

The park offers a visitor center/Arkansas Welcome Center to interpret the history of the region, and the development of the nearby city. A pavilion, picnic areas, baseball field, and playground are available for visitors as well. Seasonal boat rentals on Spring Lake can be obtained at the visitor center.

The Mammoth Spring Improvement and Water Power Company

The park is also the site of the now nonfunctioning Mammoth Spring Improvement and Water Power Company next to the dam that crosses the Spring River just south of the spring. The company was constructed in 1887. This company created a 198-foot limestone dam which formed Spring Lake. This dam initially powered a flour mill, cotton mill, and cotton gin. This property was acquired in 1925 by the Arkansas-Missouri Power Company, which constructed a hydroelectric facility that was operated until 1972. The company donated this property to the state to become part of the state park. These facilities, including the lake, are listed on the National Register of Historic Places. The remnants of the hydroelectric dam are still on display in the park.

Historic Mammoth Spring Train Depot

A short walking trail leads visitors to the restored train depot that formerly provided a connection for the city of Mammoth Spring to the Frisco Railway. Items of historical significance from the surrounding area, including a restored caboose, are on display in the museum.

Before 1957 local entrepreneur Kenneth "Bert" Bishop and his associate co-owned the Mammoth Spring Cattle Sales. It was located approximately where the tourist information center now stands. Local farmers routinely came to the site to sell livestock and other wares. These other wares included homemade walking sticks created and sold by Howard Green. Later, the Arkansas State Legislature voted to condemn the land and developed it into a state park. In 1957, the park was established. The original Frisco Depot, and 1885 Victorian train station, were restored in 1971. The depot now functions as a museum and contains artifacts and memorabilia. The depot was listed on the National Register in 1992.

The former hydroelectric plant and mill nearby allow visitors to understand the economic importance the spring had to the early inhabitants of the area.

ADDITIONAL INFORMATION

In a book this size, information can be missed, so here are a few resources available to anyone who has further questions about this area. Throughout the year, there are numerous festivals and events that locals and visitors enjoy. If you would like to know more about those, contact the chambers of commerce for more information.

Alton Chamber of Commerce
Address: P.O. Box 141
Alton, MO 65606
Email: info@altonchamber.com

Alton Branch of the Oregon County Library District
(Main Branch of the Oregon County Library District)
Address 20 Court Sq, Alton, MO 65606
Phone: (417) 778-6414
Email: altonpubliclibrary@hotmail.com

Koshkonong Branch of the Oregon County Library District
302 Diggins Street, Koshkonong, MO 65692
Phone: (417)867-5472
E-mail: koshlibrary@gmail.com

Mammoth Spring Chamber of Commerce
100 Main Street
Mammoth Spring, AR
870.625.3518

Mammoth Spring State Park
US Highway 63 S, Mammoth Spring, AR 72554 · ~

(870) 625-7364

Myrtle Branch of the Oregon County Library District
9040 V Highway, Myrtle, MO 65778
Phone: (417)938-4350
E-mail:myrtlepubliclibrary@gmail.com

Oregon County Historical Society
https://ocmohistory.wordpress.com/

Thayer Chamber of Commerce
200 E Walnut St, Thayer, MO 65791 · ~15.8 mi
(417) 264-7324

Thayer Branch of the Oregon County Library District
121 N. Second Street, Thayer, MO 65791
Phone (417)264-3091
Email: thayerpubliclibrary@gmail.com

Thomasville Branch of the Oregon County Library District
132 Old Street, Birch Tree, MO 65438
Phone: (417)764-3603
E-mail:thomasvillepubliclibrary@gmail.com

Cygnet Brown has lived in the Missouri Ozarks most of her adult life and most of that has been in Oregon County.

She is the author of the historical fiction series *The Locket Saga*. She produced her first book in 2013.

In addition to *The Locket Saga,* she has written *Because of Ryan,* a contemporary romance. She has also written several nonfiction books including *Simply Vegetable Gardening, Help from Kelp, Using Diatomaceous Earth Around the House and Yard, Living Today, The Power of Now, Write a Book and Ignite Your Business, The Survival Garden,* and most recently co-wrote *Gourmet Weeds* with Kerry Kelley also living in Oregon County.

Check out her blogs https://authorcygnetbrown.com and https://the-perpetual-homestead-er.com for the latest information about where you can learn the location of events she is attending. In addition, you can read interviews with other writers and gardeners, and learn her tips for living the homestead life in the Ozarks.